MW01173596

To

From

Date

A NOTE FROM THE AUTHOR

Thank you for picking up this one-of-a-kind devotional journal. It's truly unique because it's about to be filled with your words, your thoughts, your hopes, your dreams—you! It's about to be filled with you, and you are most definitely one of a kind.

Hi, I'm Susan Goss, and by profession, I am a licensed professional counselor and a licensed marriage and family therapist. I am also the founder and director of Tangible Truth Ministries, where we aim to creatively share God's truth through conferences, workshops, The Tangible Truth Podcast, and more. We also provide affordable mental health services for those with financial constraints.

I wrote this devotional journal to help you find your footing. It's so easy to get caught up in things we can't control, to get stuck in places we don't want to be, and to listen to and believe messages that simply aren't true. When around you the world is whirling and you don't know what to grab onto, hold on to these three things: your faith in Jesus, His unconditional love for you, and the forgiveness He promises you.

It is my hope that you'll take this opportunity to be open and honest with God. He longs for you to bring your whole self—your one-of-a-kind, unique, amazing self—to His embrace, where acceptance and love await. All you need to do is grab your pen (or pencil), invite God into the process, and write whatever comes to mind. He will take it from there.

My prayer is that you have a meaningful and
enjoyable journaling experience,

Susan Goss

faith
love
forgiveness

SUSAN GOSS

DEVOTIONAL JOURNAL

DaySpring

LIVE YOUR FAITH

Contents

Beth Moore & Susan Goss

We grew up together in Arkadelphia, Arkansas. We both attended the First Baptist Church, where each of us came to know Jesus as our personal Lord and Savior and were baptized. If the church doors were open, we went through them. Sunday morning, Sunday night, Wednesday night suppers, handbell choir, youth group, Sunday School, Training Union, Mission Friends... You name it, we did it. Mission Friends is a church group for children where they begin the journey of living a life on mission for God. And we had the best Mission Friends' teacher in the world: Mary King. Mrs. King loved Jesus and she loved us and we knew it full well. In return, we adored Mrs. King and with great anticipation looked forward to our "weekly dose" of Missions. She taught us what missions really meant and who missionaries were and how to pray for both. She taught us how to pray for other countries. And we learned all of this at such an early age . . . yet it stuck, never to be forgotten, only leaving a thirst to know more. Mrs. King even cooked different food from different countries so that we could better understand other cultures that were different from our own. Our boundless love for missionaries both here and abroad, even today, is because of the seed planted by Mary King those many years ago. There is no doubt. As the lyrics to an old familiar children's song go, "Red and yellow, black and white, they are precious in His sight. Jesus loves the little children of the world." Mrs. King left a longing in our hearts for the lost around the world to know Jesus.

What started as a seed for missions in our hometown church many years ago, under the divine placement of Mary King, has blossomed throughout our lifespan into a full-fledged passion to continually seek God's guidance for how we can be used in the effort of helping others know and love Jesus Christ.

(Side note to reader: Beth's reach is global, literally reaching the world with the truth of God through her numerous Bible studies, teachings, Living Proof live events, and prolific writing. Beth Green Moore is a David in a Goliath world.

Susan came to know Jesus as a little girl and has been talking about Him ever since. She is a licensed professional counselor, licensed marriage and family therapist, author, speaker, and podcaster who sees herself as a vessel that God can use to bring about lasting change one person, one couple, one family, one generational footprint at a time.)

When we were children in Arkadelphia, we never would have guessed what God had for us in the years ahead. We have stayed in contact for more than four decades and have a deep love and respect for each other. When you have a friendship that is rooted in faith and truth, you have something special. We both understand that we are nothing without God. We thank Him every moment for His grace and mercy—and we are in a constant state of awe that He would choose us, those two little girls from Arkansas, to bring His message of hope and encouragement to so many.

For many years we discussed the possibility of hosting a conference together, and in 2024, we decided it was time. In praying over the theme, God revealed three words to us: Faith, Love, and Forgiveness. Because in our lives, we've found that if we are relying on our faith, living in the light of His love, and forgiving ourselves as well as those who have wronged us, then we are living with joy and contentment.

It is our hope that this devotional journal will help you focus on where you truly are in these three areas. How strong is your faith? Do you feel His love for you? Are you expressing His love to those around you? Are you forgiving yourself for the past? Are you accepting God's mercy with an open heart?

One of the most wonderful things about God is . . . He doesn't expect perfection. In fact, He knows it's not possible. The two of us have not always gotten it right either. But it's in those moments when we feel unsettled, like it's all falling apart on us, that we have learned to turn to God. To have a heart-to-heart with Him. To ask Him to strengthen our faith, to fill us with His love, and to release us from the pain of unforgiveness. Maybe it's time for you to have this type of honest conversation with your Creator.

If you take nothing else away from this journaling experience, we hope you take away that you are fearfully and wonderfully made. My goodness, when asked in junior high school what we wanted to be when we grew up, Beth said she planned to be a drum majorette and Susan said she planned to be an Olympic runner . . . but God had other plans. We're all a work in progress. We're all on a journey of faith, love, and forgiveness, and it's the journey that draws us closer and closer to God . . . and we can't think of a better place to be, can you? We love you.

Beth Moore

Susan Goss

Beth Moore & Susan Goss

Cultivating Faith

Have you ever felt like God literally stopped you dead in your tracks while reading Scripture, and then you heard Him whisper in your ear something like "I want you to chew on what you just read"? A gentle yet clear assignment you knew you either must surrender to or miss out on something God was wanting to teach you. That happened to me one morning when I was reading in Psalms and got to Psalm 37:3 (NASB1995): "Trust in the LORD, and do good; dwell in the land and cultivate faithfulness." And just like that, I felt God turn my complete attention to one phrase: *cultivate faithfulness.*

What's the first thing you think of when you hear the word "cultivate"? Is it a garden? Or digging in the soil? Or maybe planting seeds under the watchful eye of a patient gardener who meticulously cultivates his harvest? Whatever "cultivate" means to you, we can all agree that it is a laborious process. In fact, Merriam Webster defines it as (1) to foster the growth of; (2) further, encourage; and (3) refine: to improve by labor, care, or study.

Are you a plant lover? Those who genuinely love to garden are usually extremely patient, very watchful, and particularly detailed. They feel protective over their seedlings, feeding and watching and fostering their growth.

In the context of Psalm 37:3, those surrounding David were complaining that others who did not love God were prospering, while they, who did love God, were suffering. This was not fair, and they were letting David know about it! David replied, "Trust in the LORD, and do good; dwell in the land and cultivate faithfulness (NASB1995)."

What I know therapeutically is that unless you are buying something and need to compare prices, comparison breeds discontentment almost 100 percent of the time. And in this case, those surrounding David were cultivating discontentment by comparing themselves to others. I can't help but think that's what David was trying to teach his companions—and what God was trying to teach me that morning.

We are cultivating something literally all the time. Have you ever thought about it that way? At times, we can even cultivate negative things like bitterness—and just like a seed that is watered, bitterness also grows. Likewise, kindness and joy can be cultivated and can grow exponentially when nurtured and cared for. And just like a master gardener cultivating plants, we can cultivate faithfulness by digging into God's Word, and we can water it by spending time with the Lord. Our roots then become planted deep in the soil of our faith so that when storms come—and they do come—we will not be washed away. It can be a laborious process but one that God desires to walk with us every step, hand in hand.

Prompt to Ponder:

When have you experienced a nudge from God but didn't act on it? What did that feel like? Process with God.

"I am the good shepherd.
I know my own and my own know me."

Prompt to Ponder:

What are you currently cultivating in your life? For example: Are you cultivating faithfulness, generosity, and thankfulness? Or are you cultivating anger and bitterness? Open your heart and process with God.

Remember this: Whoever sows sparingly will also reap sparingly,
and whoever sows generously will also reap generously.

II Corinthians 9:6 niv

Prompt to Ponder:

Our reading this week lends itself to a topic most worthy of a "mirror moment" with God. Quiet your heart and ask God: *Where am I quick to take my eyes off of You because I get so easily distracted in a world of comparison?* Be honest with God in your processing today.

For am I now seeking the approval of man, or of God?
Or am I trying to please man? If I were still trying to please man,
I would not be a servant of Christ.

Prompt to Ponder:

Do you fight comparing yourself, your children, or your family to others? Or do you perhaps struggle thinking that others have the material things, friends, or community that you wish you had? Write a list of what you really struggle with in the area of comparison and then process with God in releasing them to Him.

Each one should test their own actions.
Then they can take pride in themselves alone,
without comparing themselves to someone else.

GALATIANS 6:4 NIV

Prompt to Ponder:

Take a moment to look back at the definition of what it means to cultivate. Then ask yourself, *How am I doing that?* Spend a few quiet moments asking God how He wants you to cultivate faith, and record what He says.

_____

_____

_____

_____

_____

_____

_____

_____

_____

_____

_____

_____

_____

_____

_____

_____

_____

_____

_____

_____

_____

_____

Commit your works to the LORD,
and your plans will be established.

PROVERBS 16:3 NASB

Prompt to Ponder:

What kind of soil are you planting/cultivating your faith in? Talk to God about the kind of soil you want your life to be.

"The seed that fell among thorns stands for those who hear,
but as they go on their way they are choked by life's worries,
riches and pleasures, and they do not mature.
But the seed on good soil stands for those with a noble and good heart,
who hear the word, retain it, and by persevering produce a crop."

LUKE 8: 14–15 NIV

Prompt to Ponder:

What are you consistently watering your faith with so it will grow? If you don't feel like your faith is growing, ask the Lord to show you how He wants to nourish you.

Therefore, my beloved brothers, be steadfast, immovable,
always abounding in the work of the Lord,
knowing that in the Lord your labor is not in vain.

I CORINTHIANS 15:58 ESV

Whatever we cultivate can draw us closer to God or can become a distraction from Him.

SUSAN GOSS

The Faith It Takes to Release Control

*Cast all your anxiety on Him
because He cares for you.*

I PETER 5:7 NIV

Our Scripture today calls for action! This is not a verse of passivity. We participate with God by actively releasing, casting, turning over to Him that which is not ours to hold. As humans, we are prone to grasp for control of whatever makes us feel anxious and out of control. But this is not God's plan. He knows it's all too much, so He invites us to release our worries to Him. God can be fully trusted with each person and situation we need to let go of and release the burden of control. Why? *Because He cares for us—for me and for you.*

Yet I've never known a person, including myself, who thinks releasing control is easy. The word *control* conjures up a lot of different feelings and emotions from people—but why? I can tell you as a therapist that virtually everyone struggles with the need to control either someone or something in their life. When someone feels like they are under the control of another person in their life, the idea of control brings on deeper feelings of isolation and helplessness, loss of identity, and, painfully, sometimes even paralyzing fear. And then there are others who must go through the daunting frustration of watching a loved one being controlled by another person, substance, or situation, and lacking the ability to do anything about it. Yet as challenging as these scenarios are, we seem to have a false sense that somehow *control* equals *security*. However, over time, we soon realize nothing could be further from the truth.

By trying to control the people or circumstances

around us, our lives have become more anxiety-ridden, fear-based, chaotic, exhausting—the list could go on and on—all of which make us feel like we are *losing control*, the very opposite of being *in control*.

But God tells us to release our burdens, situations, and the people in our lives to Him because *we were never designed to carry His load*.

Playing God is an exhausting role. I know, I've tried it and failed miserably. And as ridiculous as it may sound, have you ever tried to tell God what to do? Sadly, I've tried this approach with God also, and you might not be surprised when I tell you, that doesn't work either. We may not readily own up to trying to play God, but when we act before we seek God's wisdom, we in essence take on the role that was meant for God alone. That would explain how, before too long, we become burdened and weighed down, feeling the weight of the world on our shoulders! We're trying to control everything and everyone, and it's exhausting. It is simply not our business to do so.

Yet something amazing happens when we accept God's call to release our grip of control and surrender our anxiety to Him: transformation. This process ignites a metamorphosis of sorts—we are radically changed when we go from a **me-controlled heart** to a **God-controlled heart**.

God knows all things. He is steady, secure, and safe. What a gift that we can trust Him with *all things* and have faith that He will do what is best.

By learning to release control to God, we begin a faith journey of trust that leads to a deeper abiding in Christ than we have ever known. And we gain this deeper abiding, ironically, by letting go.

Prompt to Ponder:

Think of a time when you chose to *depend on your own understanding* without seeking God first. How did that work out? What has God been teaching you about the value of His wisdom?

Trust in the Lord with all your heart;
do not depend on your own understanding.
Seek His will in all you do, and He will show you which path to take.
Don't be impressed with your own wisdom.
Instead, fear the Lord and turn away from evil.

PROVERBS 3:5–7 NLT

Prompt to Ponder:

What are potential barriers that keep you from releasing control? How might God help you to overcome those barriers?

_____

_____

_____

_____

_____

_____

_____

_____

_____

_____

_____

_____

_____

_____

_____

_____

_____

_____

_____

_____

_____

_____

_____

_____

_____

_____

_____

Jesus looked at them intently and said, "Humanly speaking,
it is impossible. But with God everything is possible."

MATTHEW 19:26 NLT

Prompt to Ponder:

Consider today's Scripture on faith (see bottom of next page). How does this affect your ability to release control to God and trust Him with the people and circumstances in your life you are currently trying to fix or change?

Now faith is the certainty of things hoped for,
a proof of things not seen.

HEBREWS 11:1 NASB

Prompt to Ponder:

God tells us to come to Him, and He will give us rest for our souls. Describe a time when you *let go* and *let God* work in a situation you had no control over. How did coming to Him instead of forging ahead on your own make a difference?

"Come to Me, all you who are weary and burdened, and I will give you rest.
Take My yoke upon you and learn from Me,
for I am gentle and humble in heart,
and you will find rest for your souls.
For My yoke is easy and My burden is light."

MATTHEW 11:28–30 NIV

Prompt to Ponder:

What would it feel like to have peace that seems to make no sense? How would you recognize it? Write out a prayer of thanksgiving and release to God.

Do not be anxious about anything, but in every situation,
by prayer and petition, with thanksgiving, present your requests to God.
And the peace of God, which transcends all understanding,
will guard your hearts and your minds in Christ Jesus.

PHILIPPIANS 4:6–7 NIV

Prompt to Ponder:

We can practice releasing our cares to God because of His promises to strengthen, help, and uphold us. Knowing this promise, explain how the process of releasing control will be easier for you.

"So do not fear, for I am with you;
do not be dismayed, for I am your God.
I will strengthen you and help you;
I will uphold you with my righteous right hand."

ISAIAH 41:10 NIV

Prompt to Ponder:

Identify a person or situation God is calling you to entrust to Him. How will keeping your thoughts fixed on God strengthen your faith and trust in Him?

You will keep in perfect peace all who trust in You,
all whose thoughts are fixed on You!
Trust in the LORD always,
for the LORD GOD is the eternal Rock.

ISAIAH 26:3–4 NLT

We were never designed to carry God's load.

SUSAN GOSS

An Act of Faith

I have fought the good fight, I have finished the race, I have kept the faith.
Now there is in store for me the crown of righteousness, which the Lord,
the righteous Judge, will award to me on that day—and not only to me,
but also to all who have longed for his appearing.

II TIMOTHY 4:7–8 NIV

*W*hen peace like a river attendeth my way, when sorrows like sea billows roll; whatever my lot, Thou hast taught me to say, "It is well, it is well with my soul." These words are from the well-known hymn "It Is Well with My Soul," penned by Horatio Gates Spafford after experiencing great tragedy in his life. Spafford and his wife, Anna, had five children: four daughters and a son. At age four, their son died suddenly of scarlet fever. Only two years later, a trip to England was planned for the family, but Spafford was delayed in leaving, due to business demands. Anna and the girls went on with Spafford's blessing, and he would join as soon as he possibly could. While crossing the Atlantic on their steamship, *Ville du Havre*, their vessel was struck by an iron sailing ship and sank. All four of Horatio Spafford's daughters lost their lives. Miraculously, Anna survived.

After hearing of the devastating news of his daughters, yet hopeful to reconnect with his wife, Spafford began his seaward journey. While traveling, he was informed by the captain that their vessel was crossing over the exact spot where the *Ville du Havre* had sunk. This is when it is said that Spafford stopped, remembering the love he shared with his four beautiful daughters, and began to pen the words to "It Is Well with My Soul."

Spafford's story of unbearable pain and suffering, mingled with unwavering faith and unexplainable peace, gives one a perfect image of II Corinthians 5:7: "Our life is lived by faith. We do not live by what we see in front of us" (paraphrase). But it's so much easier to look at what's in front of you, right? When we face certain trials, tragedies, and devastating loss, it's human nature to see what is in front of us and sometimes think God is far away or has forgotten us. Yet, He is near and even promises to never leave us or forsake us. It's a promise. God is where you are right now. Whether in the middle of a tragedy or in the middle of a celebration, God is there with you.

When we don't know what else to do, we can trust in the promises of God. Sometimes it helps to say them out loud. Here are a few examples: God promises that nothing can separate you from Him (Romans 8:38–39); God promises to be with you (Joshua 1:5, 9); God promises eternal life (John 3:16). One way to look at faith is giving to God what we don't know or understand because He knows *everything*, and we can trust Him to do what's best.

A faith like this is the only way Horatio Spafford, after such horrific loss, could have written lyrics expressing a sense of well-being during such a time of profound grief. Truly, God gives a peace that surpasses all understanding. He is a faithful God.

Prompt to Ponder:

Reflect on a time when you faced uncertainty or challenges in your life. How did you maintain hope and faith during that period?

_____

_____

_____

_____

_____

_____

_____

_____

_____

_____

_____

_____

_____

_____

_____

_____

_____

_____

_____

_____

_____

_____

_____

_____

_____

_____

Let us hold tightly without wavering to the hope we affirm,
for God can be trusted to keep His promise.

Prompt to Ponder:

Reflect on a time when you faced a moral or spiritual decision. How did your commitment (or lack of commitment) to God's ways influence your choices?

_____

_____

_____

_____

_____

_____

_____

_____

_____

_____

_____

_____

_____

_____

_____

_____

_____

_____

_____

_____

_____

_____

_____

_____

_____

I have chosen the way of faithfulness;
I have set my heart on Your laws.

PSALM 119:30 NIV

Prompt to Ponder:

Describe your journey of enduring through trials and what you've learned about resilience, patience, and trusting in God's plan?

Consider it pure joy, my brothers and sisters,
whenever you face trials of many kinds,
because you know that the testing of your faith produces perseverance.
Let perseverance finish its work so that you may be
mature and complete, not lacking anything.

JAMES 1:2–4 NIV

Prompt to Ponder:

Write out a list of actions you can take today to promote justice, show kindness, and embrace humility in your relationship with God. (Refer to the Scripture on the bottom of the next page.)

He has told you, O man, what is good;
and what does the Lord require of you but to do justice,
to love kindness, and to walk humbly with your God?

MICAH 6:8 ESV

Prompt to Ponder:

How could you encourage yourself and others to stand firm in the faith today? What does standing firm look like to you?

_____

_____

_____

_____

_____

_____

_____

_____

_____

_____

_____

_____

_____

_____

_____

_____

_____

_____

_____

_____

_____

_____

_____

_____

Be on guard. Stand firm in the faith.
Be courageous. Be strong.

I Corinthians 16:13 nlt

Prompt to Ponder:

Several promises of God were mentioned in the devotion this week (see page 44). Is there one that has special meaning to you? Explain. Why do you suppose His promises can function as our armor and protection?

He will cover you with His feathers. He will shelter you with His wings.
His faithful promises are your armor and protection.

PSALM 91:4 NLT

Prompt to Ponder:

As you remember the devotion from earlier this week (page 44) and consider today's Scripture (bottom of the next page), what comes up for you? How has your faith grown?

And those who know Your name will put their trust in You,
For You, LORD, have not abandoned those who seek You.

PSALM 9:10 NASB

FAITH means giving to **God** what we don't know or understand because **He** knows what we don't know, and **He** understands what we don't understand. **He** knows *everything*, and we can trust **God** to do what's best.

SUSAN GOSS

I Love You If . . .

For this is how God loved the world:
He gave His one and only Son,
so that everyone who believes in Him
will not perish but have eternal life.

JOHN 3:16 NLT

We all received different messages from our families of origin when we were growing up. We are all products of how we were raised—both good and bad. Some may have received messages associated with love that were conditional, messages like, *I'll love you if you do what I tell you to do*; and then if you didn't, that love was withheld. One soon learns in that environment: *If I please and achieve, I am loved; if I don't, I am not.* That kind of love is conditional. In therapy we might call this "performance-based relationships" or "performance-based love." In these relationships there is a fear of losing one's true identity when love is based on whether performance is good or bad. For instance, if performance is good, the message is, "You are good, and I love you." If the performance is bad, the message is, "You are bad, and I don't love you." However, the message of unconditional love simply says, *I love you—period! No conditions. I love you for who you are, not for what you do.*

Unconditional love is not a quid pro quo agreement between two people. It gives without expecting anything in return. Unconditional love endures through every circumstance and never gives up!

Christ was, is, and will always be the ultimate and perfect example of what unconditional love looks like. He never once said to anyone, "Go get your life cleaned up first and then you can come follow Me." To the tax collector that everyone despised,

He said, "Let's have dinner" (Luke 5:27–32). To the Samaritan woman going to a well to draw water at an inconspicuous time of day so that no one would see her, He not only spoke to her, He also told her things about herself that only she would have known, opening the door for Jesus to share about the true living water that would allow her to never thirst again (John 4:7–26). Jesus exudes love because He is love!

I remember growing up learning about how much Jesus loved me. I remember learning that He loved me just as I was and that I didn't have to earn His love because He already loved me completely. I didn't have to prove anything to Him. I didn't have to walk on eggshells, worrying if I was going to get it "right." I could be me and trust that God loved me. It was like a huge burden lifted from my little eight-year-old body. I could relax with Jesus knowing He loved me—no ifs, no shoulds, no strings attached. I simply could not stop talking about Jesus. I still can't! That's how unconditional love works; it makes you feel relaxed . . . safe . . . loved.

Prompt to Ponder:

Rewrite this very familiar passage from God's Word and personalize it.

"For God so loved (your name) that He gave (your name) His only begotten Son, that (your name) shall not perish, but have eternal life."

Read it out loud. What thoughts come up for you as you read this verse with your own name?

*"For God so loved the world, that He gave His only begotten Son,
that whoever believes in Him shall not perish, but have eternal life."*

JOHN 3:16 NASB1995

Prompt to Ponder:

When you approach God, do you begin to relax knowing He is a safe place of rest for you? Why or why not?

*For the Lord G*OD*, the Holy One of Israel, has said:*
"You will be delivered by returning and resting; your strength will lie
in quiet confidence. But you are not willing."

ISAIAH 30:15 CSB

Prompt to Ponder:

Is there something in your life that feels like it is separating you from God's love? Talk to Him about it.

_____

_____

_____

_____

_____

_____

_____

_____

_____

_____

_____

_____

_____

_____

_____

_____

_____

_____

_____

_____

_____

_____

_____

_____

_____

_____

_____

_____

Who shall separate us from the love of Christ? Shall tribulation, or distress,
or persecution, or famine, or nakedness, or danger, or sword? . . .
No, in all these things we are more than conquerors through him who loved us.
For I am sure that neither death nor life, nor angels nor rulers, nor things present
nor things to come, nor powers, nor height nor depth, nor anything else in all
creation, will be able to separate us from the love of God in Christ Jesus our Lord.

ROMANS 8:35, 37–39 ESV

Prompt to Ponder:

What was the message of love that you received growing up? Would you identify it more as conditional love or unconditional love? Share more about that.

Dear friends, let us continue to love one another,
for love comes from God.
Anyone who loves is a child of God and knows God.
But anyone who does not love does not know God, for God is love.

I JOHN 4:7–8 NLT

Prompt to Ponder:

God's unconditional love and His attentive thoughts toward you have no end.
How does that make you feel?

How precious also are Your thoughts for me, God!
How vast is the sum of them!
Were I to count them, they would outnumber the sand.
When I awake, I am still with You.

PSALM 139:17–18 NASB

Prompt to Ponder:

If Christ models unconditional love for us, how can we show that same love to those around us? Some examples might be making a meal for your neighbors who are new parents, spending time with the elderly at your local nursing home, or asking what you can do to serve in your local church. Ask God to show you who He wants you to love this week and how. Write down what He's stirring in your heart.

"So now I am giving you a new commandment: Love each other.
Just as I have loved you, you should love each other."

JOHN 13:34 NLT

Prompt to Ponder:

Is your identity firmly found in Christ? Or have you let others tell you who you are? Process this critical question with God.

My old self has been crucified with Christ.
It is no longer I who live, but Christ lives in me.

GALATIANS 2:20 NLT

Unconditional love says: I love you for who you are, not for what you do.

SUSAN GOSS

The Love Race

And do everything with love.

I CORINTHIANS 16:14 NLT

In 1992, British athlete Derek Redmond was set for the race of his life in the 400-meter semifinals at the Barcelona Olympics. He had already won his first-round heat and quarterfinal and was poised for another win. In lane five, Derek had a great start out of the blocks, running with the focus of being the winner as he crossed the finish line. But fifteen seconds into the race, something happened: a deafening pop and an abrupt stop, and Derek went down as he grabbed hold of his right hamstring in anguish. Officials started moving toward him. Yet despite excruciating pain, with the determination of a true Olympian, he waved them away as he struggled to get upright and began hobbling around the track to the finish line with the same focus as he started the race.

Then a most familiar voice made its way through all the noise and the officials. Derek said in an interview: "I had held it together until I heard his voice, and when I knew it was my dad, I lost it. This man has been alongside me my whole life . . . supporting me . . . sacrificing . . . and when I heard his voice, I knew I could let down." His dad said, "You're a champion: you've got nothing to prove." Derek said at that moment, "Dad, I want to finish, get me back in the semifinal." His dad replied, "Okay. We started this thing together, and now we'll finish it together." Together Derek and his dad crossed the finish line in the world's greatest competition.

Sometimes it's about so much more than the competition itself, isn't it? All the hours, the years of training, the regimen, the laser focus, and the sacrifices made along the way. When Derek heard his father's voice, felt his father's touch, he was safe. Derek's father loved his son unconditionally, and his son knew that and felt safe in his father's arms.

That's the kind of love God has for us too. And just like Derek, when we fall, feel defeated, or find ourselves racked with pain, struggling to find our way back up, Jesus meets us. And like Derek's father, God puts His loving, comforting arms around us to hold us up and let us know we're not alone. Jesus stays close and walks with us, letting us lean on Him for every step. Whether we're crawling, walking, or running, God is by our side. There is not a pace too slow or too fast for God. You can't outrun Him, and you can't outwait Him. His love is unconditional, and His arms are safe.

Prompt to Ponder:

Derek's dad told him he had "nothing to prove." Do you find yourself trying to prove something to yourself or others? And if so, for who and for what reason? Ask God to help you process this.

Each time he said, "My grace is all you need.
My power works best in weakness." So now I am glad to boast
about my weaknesses, so that the power of Christ can work through me.
That's why I take pleasure in my weaknesses, and in the insults,
hardships, persecutions, and troubles that I suffer for Christ.
For when I am weak, then I am strong.

II Corinthians 12:9–10 nlt

Prompt to Ponder:

When being interviewed Derek said, "The key to falling in a race is getting back up. No matter how many times it takes, get back up." This kind of perseverance is possible when we rely on God's strength. Where in your life do you need to turn to Christ and ask Him to strengthen you?

For I can do everything through Christ,
who gives me strength.

PHILIPPIANS 4:13 NLT

Prompt to Ponder:

Do you feel like you are running the race of life on autopilot or with purpose? We all get the same twenty-four hours in a day, but the outcome can be vastly different based on our focus and intention. Ask God what it would look like for you to "run in such a way that you may win" this week. Record what you hear.

Do you not know that those who run in a race all run,
but only one receives the prize? Run in such a way that you may win.

I CORINTHIANS 9:24 NASB

Prompt to Ponder:

What does "unconditional love" mean to you? How have you seen God's love for
the world and for you personally on display?

God demonstrates His own love for us in this:
While we were still sinners, Christ died for us.

ROMANS 5:8 NIV

DAY 5

Prompt to Ponder:

Think about your relationships (friends, family, coworkers, and yes, even God).
Which ones feel safe? List the reasons why.

This I declare about the LORD: He alone is my refuge,
my place of safety; He is my God, and I trust Him.

PSALM 91:2 NLT

Prompt to Ponder:

Like Derek's devastating injury that happened so suddenly, have you ever experienced an unexpected event that changed the course of your life either forever or temporarily? Explain. How did you respond?

_____

_____

_____

_____

_____

_____

_____

_____

_____

_____

_____

_____

_____

_____

_____

_____

_____

_____

_____

_____

_____

_____

"I have told you all this so that you may have peace in Me.
Here on earth you will have many trials and sorrows.
But take heart, because I have overcome the world."

JOHN 16:33 NLT

Prompt to Ponder:

Write about a time you showed someone unconditional love so they could feel safe and not alone. In return, what impact did it have on you when someone loved you unconditionally?

_____

_____

_____

_____

_____

_____

_____

_____

_____

_____

_____

_____

_____

_____

_____

_____

_____

_____

_____

_____

_____

_____

_____

"So now I am giving you a new commandment:
Love each other. Just as I have loved you, you should love each other.
Your love for one another will prove to the world that you are My disciples."

Unconditional love expects nothing, and simply says *I love you, period.*

SUSAN GOSS

Love Shows Up

Dear children, let us not love with words or speech
but with actions and in truth.

1 JOHN 3:18 NIV

What I have come to know as a therapist (and human) is that one of the best ways, if not *the* best way, to connect with someone is to let them know you care by creating a "safe zone" for them. You do this by sitting and listening (without reprimand or judgment), not trying to correct, fix, or change them—just listening and letting them know they have been heard, understood, and seen. What this really involves is learning how to meet people where they are. Meet them in their greatest joy or deepest pain.

At times when words are elusive and you don't know what to say, just acknowledge, "I don't know what to say to you right now, but what I do know is that I want to be here for you." When you are able to say that to another person, they immediately feel connected to you, understood by you, and safe; they don't feel alone anymore. This fosters a sense of belonging . . . like family.

God has His own version of "meeting people where they are," and it's found in Romans 12:15 (NASB): "Rejoice with those who rejoice, and weep with those who weep." This extraordinary passage of Scripture implies that if there is reason to celebrate, then celebrate joyfully. And if there is reason for weeping, then weep and do so deeply. God is the Creator and Author of all emotions, which are meant to be felt and expressed both as individuals and together in community.

First John 3:18 reinforces this call to love one another fully. John writes, "Dear children, let us not love with words or speech but with actions and in truth" (NIV). In modern-day language, another way of saying this verse might be: Love shows up! I experienced this on a very personal level not long ago, when my mother passed away. God's own people were in fact the hands and feet of Jesus to me and my family in very practical ways. They met me where I was in my grief and supplied my needs, some of which I didn't even know I had. And if they didn't know what to say or do, they prayed or sent a gift card or brought my favorite coffee to me or delivered food or sent a text of encouragement. The list goes on and on because *love shows up*—in many ways and in different forms. It sacrifices for those it serves.

The more we look beyond ourselves, the closer we connect to others and to God. So the gift of serving is really a reflection of our love for God spilled out to others so they can see Him more clearly.

Prompt to Ponder:

Who in your life creates "safe zones" for you? Process your thoughts with God and write about them.

_____

_____

_____

_____

_____

_____

_____

_____

_____

_____

_____

_____

_____

_____

_____

_____

_____

_____

_____

_____

_____

_____

_____

_____

_____

Blessed be the God and Father of our Lord Jesus Christ,
the Father of mercies and God of all comfort, who comforts us
in all our affliction so that we will be able to comfort those who are in
any affliction with the comfort with which we ourselves are comforted by God.

II Corinthians 1:3-4 NASB1995

Prompt to Ponder:

Continuing on from yesterday's journaling process with God on "safe zones" . . .
Ask yourself: Are you good at creating "safe zones" for those who need a place
of refuge? Describe a time you created a safe zone for someone and they were
able to open up to you.

Jesus wept.

JOHN 11:35 NASB

Prompt to Ponder:

Where in your life have you been wanting to "show" love but have been afraid to step out, for fear of rejection? Process this with God and write about it below.

Dear children, let's not merely say that we love each other;
let us show the truth by our actions.

I JOHN 3:18 NLT

Prompt to Ponder:

Do you live your life like love is a noun (a feeling), a verb (an action), or both? Process this with God and jot down your thoughts.

But be doers of the Word,
and not hearers only, deceiving yourselves.

JAMES 1:22 ESV

Prompt to Ponder:

Knowing that God always looks at the motives of our heart, process with God today the "why" behind what you do for others. What's your motivation—is it to please God or man?

People may be pure in their own eyes,
but the LORD examines their motives.

PROVERBS 16:2 NLT

Prompt to Ponder:

Consider the gift it is for God's light to shine through you. Think about the last time you recognized that you were shining for Jesus. Write about what happened and how it felt. Then read it back to God.

Let your light shine before men in such a way
that they may see your good works,
and glorify your Father who is in heaven.

Matthew 5:16 nasb1995

Prompt to Ponder:

When was the last time you were the love that showed up for someone else?
Process this with God. Journal about it for reference later.

Love from the center of who you are, don't fake it.
Run for dear life from evil;
hold on for dear life to good.
Be good friends who love deeply;
practice playing second fiddle.

ROMANS 12:10 THE MESSAGE

Love is large and incredibly patient.

Love is gentle and consistently kind to all.

It refuses to be jealous when blessing comes

to someone else. Love does not brag about one's

achievements nor inflate its own importance.

Love does not traffic in shame and disrespect,

nor selfishly seek its own honor. Love is not eas-

ily irritated or quick to take offense. Love joyfully

celebrates honesty and finds no delight in what is

wrong. Love is a safe place of shelter, for it

never stops believing the best for others.

Love never takes failure as defeat,

for it never gives up.

I CORINTHIANS 13:4–7 TPT

A Supernatural Forgiveness

Be gentle and ready to forgive; never hold grudges. Remember,
the Lord forgave you, so you must forgive others.

COLOSSIANS 3:13 TLB

L ouis "Louie" Zamperini lived out an incredible story of forgiveness. In high school, Louie was a phenomenal runner, earning a spot on the 1936 US Olympic Team in Berlin running in the 5,000 meter race. He finished eighth in the race, but because of his performance during the final lap, he was awarded a new lap record. He was set to run again in the 1940 Olympics in Tokyo, but when World War II started, Louie began training to be a bombardier in the United States Army Air Corps.

Louie served as a bombardier on B-24 Liberators in the Pacific. On one of his search-and-rescue missions, his plane crashed into the ocean. Louie and a few of his surviving comrades began fighting for their lives, drifting on a life raft at sea. Most died of starvation and injuries from the crash. After forty-seven days on the open water, Louie, barely alive, was captured by the Japanese navy.

Louie became a prisoner of war (POW) in the Japanese war camps where he was tortured and deprived of food, water, and medical care. He was brutally beaten, interrogated, and routinely humiliated. And because Louie was an Olympian, he was transferred, to be under the watch of The Bird—the nickname of Sergeant Mutsuhiro Watanabe. The Bird became Louie's personal torturer until the war ended, two years after his plane crashed into the sea.

When Louie returned home, his healing journey was

slow and hard. During that journey he met and married Cynthia Applewhite. Although in love, he fell into alcoholism while fighting the deep wounds of post-traumatic stress disorder, which had never been treated. His marriage was failing, yet Cynthia convinced Louie to attend a Billy Graham crusade in Los Angeles. While listening to Billy Graham preach, he accepted Jesus into his life.

Everything changed that night for Louie. He stopped drinking and restored his marriage. Then he did something even more remarkable—something not natural but supernatural. He began the process of forgiving those who had captured and brutally tortured him every single day for two years . . . including the one called The Bird.

Louie's life was forever changed when Jesus entered his heart—broken as it was—and made him new.

We are never more like Christ than when we choose to forgive someone who has wronged us. Forgiveness isn't a natural thing for us to do—it is a supernatural process that we do with God's help. And the good news is, He designed us to need Him. As we see in Louie's story, forgiveness is not dependent on a certain response from the offender. It is dependent on Jesus freeing us to be who He created us to be, fully and completely—free from the bonds of anger, resentfulness, bitterness, judgment, retaliation, and revenge. With Jesus as his Savior, Louie could be at peace.

When we don't know how to begin to forgive, we can trust that Jesus does. We have a Savior who is gentle and kind, and He knows every detail of our past and every thought in our mind. Jesus will guide us in every step through forgiveness. God changes the heart. He alone brings peace that we cannot understand.

Prompt to Ponder:

When someone harms you or a person you love, do you find it hard to forgive? Process your answer honestly with God.

Be kind to each other, tenderhearted, forgiving one another,
just as God through Christ has forgiven you.

EPHESIANS 4:32 NLT

Prompt to Ponder:

Is there someone who has wronged you whom you have never fully forgiven, never fully released to God? Write about what's holding you back from forgiving.

*"When you pray, if you remember anyone who has wronged you,
forgive him so that God above can also forgive you."*

MARK 11:25 THE VOICE

Prompt to Ponder:

After reading about all that Louie Zamperini endured as a POW (see page 116), how powerful was it for you to read that he forgave—pardoned the offenses—of those who tortured him every day for two years? How does that impact your view of forgiveness?

_____

_____

_____

_____

_____

_____

_____

_____

_____

_____

_____

_____

_____

_____

_____

_____

_____

_____

_____

_____

_____

*"For if you forgive other people when they sin against you,
your heavenly Father will also forgive you."*

MATTHEW 6:14 NIV

Prompt to Ponder:

Think of a time when you have offended or wronged someone. Spend time with God processing your answer.

_____

_____

_____

_____

_____

_____

_____

_____

_____

_____

_____

_____

_____

_____

_____

_____

_____

_____

_____

_____

_____

_____

_____

_____

_____

Be gracious to me, God, according to Your faithfulness;
according to the greatness of Your compassion, wipe out my wrongdoings.
Wash me thoroughly from my guilt and cleanse me from my sin.

PSALM 51:1–2 NASB

Prompt to Ponder:

What does it mean to you that God cleanses you from all unrighteousness? If there is a sin you need to confess to the Lord, take this opportunity to do so. His faithfulness and forgiveness are yours.

If we confess our sins, he is faithful and just to forgive us
our sins and to cleanse us from all unrighteousness.

I John 1:9 esv

Prompt to Ponder:

Have you ever been forgiven when you didn't deserve it? Describe the overflowing love and gratitude that comes from being forgiven.

_____

_____

_____

_____

_____

_____

_____

_____

_____

_____

_____

_____

_____

_____

_____

_____

_____

_____

_____

_____

_____

_____

_____

_____

*"For this reason I say to you, her sins,
which are many, have been forgiven,
for she loved much; but the one
who is forgiven little, loves little."*

LUKE 7:47 NASB

Prompt to Ponder:

Jesus teaches His disciples "The Lord's Prayer" as a model for their own prayers (see Matthew 6:9-13 at the bottom of the next page). What does this model prayer mean to you? Consider speaking it back to God.

"Our Father which art in heaven, Hallowed be thy name.
Thy kingdom come, Thy will be done in earth, as it is in heaven.
Give us this day our daily bread. And forgive us our debts, as we forgive our debtors.
And lead us not into temptation, but deliver us from evil: For thine is the kingdom,
and the power, and the glory, for ever. Amen."

MATTHEW 6:9–13 KJV

We are never more like Christ than when we choose to forgive someone who has wronged us.

SUSAN GOSS

Heart Health

Above all else, guard your heart,
for everything you do flows from it.

PROVERBS 4:23 NIV

Have you ever seen a wild animal trapped in a cage? That's an image of unforgiveness. Like an animal who can't break free from the temporary prison it was never intended for, so too can we become trapped in a cage of anger, resentment, bitterness, or hate toward someone who has harmed us. And sometimes we even struggle to forgive ourselves. So how do we break free from this cage? The key is forgiveness.

Forgiveness is not just a single decision, it's a process and a way of life, and it is essential for our emotional and spiritual well-being. Although it's not easy, forgiveness can eventually bring a peace to the soul that we long for. Likewise, forgiveness unlocks the door to deep joy that only Christ can give.

Therapeutically, it has become part of my practice when working with those struggling with depression, in particular, to assess for unforgiveness. It has been my experience that many times, where there is depression, you will find unforgiveness at some level. Forgiveness work is a process that takes effort and intentionality on the part of the person wanting healing and freedom in their life. It is a day-to-day process with God of releasing the offender. Some may quickly say, "I have forgiven," thinking that a one-time decision to forgive is all they need to do, but they soon find out that their heart is still at war. True healing requires time, patience, and a daily rhythm of releasing the offense to God until the heart feels free once again.

Interestingly, a Harvard study about depression and forgiveness by Dr. Tyler VanderWeele from the Initiative on Health, Religion, and Spirituality at the Harvard T.H. Chan School of Public Health says, "Practicing forgiveness can have powerful health benefits. Observational studies, and even some randomized trials, suggest that forgiveness is associated with lower levels of depression, anxiety, and hostility; reduced substance abuse; higher self-esteem; and greater life satisfaction."

Many in the therapeutic community would say the healthiest people are those who learn how to forgive as offenses come their way, not allowing those offenses to grow, causing more bitterness and anger toward themselves or others. In order to protect and guard our heart and keep it healthy while living in this imperfect world, our heart requires proper care. Forgiveness is the key to heart health. As our Scripture states, the heart is "the source of life," and that includes our spiritual and emotional health.

I firmly believe our relationships are as healthy as we are individually. The healthiest people don't hold a grudge. Why? Because you can't guard or protect your heart and hold a grudge at the same time. Forgiveness keeps the heart healthy.

Prompt to Ponder:

Have you ever felt trapped in a confined space, a relationship, or a circumstance you could not get out of? Describe how you felt and if you were aware of God's presence.

The Lord is close to the brokenhearted
and saves those who are crushed in spirit.

PSALM 34:18 NIV

Prompt to Ponder:

Is there someone in your life whom you need to forgive? If so, what has been holding you back from forgiving them? Process this with God today as you journal.

"Do not judge, and you will not be judged.
Do not condemn, and you will not be condemned.
Forgive, and you will be forgiven."

LUKE 6:37 NIV

Prompt to Ponder:

Describe a time when you did choose to forgive someone who wronged you and what that did to your heart.

_____

_____

_____

_____

_____

_____

_____

_____

_____

_____

_____

_____

_____

_____

_____

_____

_____

_____

_____

_____

_____

_____

_____

_____

_____

Confess your sins to each other and pray for each other
so that you may be healed. The earnest prayer of a righteous person
has great power and produces wonderful results.

<small>JAMES 5:16 NLT</small>

Prompt to Ponder:

How can you start guarding and/or protecting your heart? Process this with God and begin journaling practical ways today.

Get rid of all bitterness, rage and anger,
brawling and slander, along with every form of malice.
Be kind and compassionate to one another,
forgiving each other, just as in Christ God forgave you.

Ephesians 4:31–32 NIV

Prompt to Ponder:

What are your thoughts about depression and unforgiveness being linked together?

When the righteous cry for help,
the Lord hears and delivers them out of all their troubles.

Psalm 34:17 esv

Prompt to Ponder:

How often do you seek to offer or receive forgiveness? How do you think forgiveness fosters spiritual and emotional health?

One who conceals his wrongdoings will not prosper,
but one who confesses and abandons them will find compassion.

PROVERBS 28:13 NASB

Prompt to Ponder:

What do you think about the statement, "Our relationships are as healthy as we are individually"? What does this quote have to do with forgiveness versus unforgiveness?

_____

_____

_____

_____

_____

_____

_____

_____

_____

_____

_____

_____

_____

_____

_____

_____

_____

_____

_____

_____

_____

_____

_____

_____

_____

Put on then, as God's chosen ones, holy and beloved,
compassionate hearts, kindness, humility, meekness, and patience,
bearing with one another and, if one has a complaint against another,
forgiving each other; as the Lord has forgiven you, so you also must forgive.

COLOSSIANS 3:12–13 ESV

True healing requires time, patience, and a daily rhythm of releasing the offense to God until the heart feels free once again.

SUSAN GOSS

Honest Feelings

Love prospers when a fault is forgiven,
but dwelling on it separates close friends.

PROVERBS 17:9 NLT

Forgiveness researcher Robert Enright says, "Forgiving begins with acknowledging that we are people who have a right to be treated with respect. Forgiving does not require denying that we have been hurt. On the contrary, to forgive we have to admit that we have been hurt and that we have a right to feel hurt, angry, or resentful. Forgiving does not require denying our feelings." This is such a powerful quote because it validates our right to feel what we are feeling. When we acknowledge our wounds, we can better understand the emotions that are attached to our pain. In doing this, we are able to identify, with true honesty, what or who we need to forgive.

My grandmother used to say, "I wouldn't sweep that under the rug . . . it might come back to bite you." And I would now add, "If you sweep stuff under the rug long enough, eventually you'll start tripping over it." In my therapy sessions I might use different terminology, but I definitely affirm the intent of my grandmother's wisdom. If we deny our hurt and push our feelings away where we don't have to immediately deal with them, over time the hurt will accumulate.

God always wants us to be honest about our feelings. After all, He created us with a full spectrum of emotions. David reminds us in Psalm 139:4 that God already knows what is on our tongue before we speak it, which implies we are to be totally transparent with God. You can't shock God, He knows everything. When we are able to admit our true feelings and process them with God—whether beginning a journey of forgiving ourselves or someone who has wronged us—that is when we are able to genuinely begin the healing process. Although God doesn't always swoop in and rescue us when we are in the middle of our hurt and pain, He never leaves our side as we walk through it. We are never alone. The psalmist reminds us in Psalm 139:7–10 that there is nowhere we can go that God is not already there. God meets us where we are and will never leave us or forsake us.

My granddaughter was given an award at school with very poignant words written on the certificate: "Forgiveness: deciding that someone who has wronged you doesn't have to pay." Wow! What a fabulous award and one that took me by surprise, in the best of ways. Learning the value of forgiving someone who has wronged you at an early age helps grow a heart full of compassion and grace. Through Christ we can receive such an award. It is found in John 3:16 (NIV): "For God so loved the world that He gave His one and only Son, that whoever believes in Him shall not perish but have eternal life."

Prompt to Ponder:

When have you been guilty of sweeping your feelings under the rug? What was the result of refusing to talk about, acknowledge, or process your emotions or experience?

_____

_____

_____

_____

_____

_____

_____

_____

_____

_____

_____

_____

_____

_____

_____

_____

_____

_____

_____

_____

_____

_____

_____

Oh, what joy for those whose disobedience is forgiven,
whose sin is put out of sight!
Yes, what joy for those whose record the Lord
has cleared of guilt, whose lives are lived in complete honesty!

PSALM 32:1-2 NLT

Prompt to Ponder:

Write out what these words mean to you personally: "Forgiveness: deciding that someone who has wronged you doesn't have to pay."

_____

_____

_____

_____

_____

_____

_____

_____

_____

_____

_____

_____

_____

_____

_____

_____

_____

_____

_____

_____

_____

_____

_____

_____

_____

"And I will forgive their wickedness,
and I will never again remember their sins."

HEBREWS 8:12 NLT

Prompt to Ponder:

Look again at Robert Enright's quote from this week's devotion: "Forgiving begins with acknowledging that we are people who have a right to be treated with respect. Forgiving does not require denying that we have been hurt. On the contrary, to forgive we have to admit that we have been hurt and that we have a right to feel hurt, angry, or resentful. Forgiving does not require denying our feelings." What might it look like to accept your own feelings for what they are instead of denying them?

As far as the east is from the west,
so far has He removed our wrongdoings from us.

PSALM 103:12 NASB

Prompt to Ponder:

Where in your life have you experienced God's unfailing love? If you're in need of help today, write out an honest prayer and thank God for His faithfulness and forgiveness.

O Lord, You are so good, so ready to forgive,
so full of unfailing love for all who ask for Your help.

PSALM 86:5 NLT

Prompt to Ponder:

What holds you back from forgiving?

Then Peter came to Him and asked,
"Lord, how often should I forgive someone who sins against me? Seven times?"
"No, not seven times," Jesus replied, "but seventy times seven!"

MATTHEW 18:21–22 NLT

Prompt to Ponder:

Do you sometimes struggle to forgive yourself, even when you know God has forgiven you? Process this with God today.

_____
_____
_____
_____
_____
_____
_____
_____
_____
_____
_____
_____
_____
_____
_____
_____
_____
_____
_____
_____
_____
_____
_____
_____
_____
_____
_____

"I—yes, I alone—will blot out your sins
for my own sake and will never think of them again."

ISAIAH 43:25 NLT

Prompt to Ponder:

What does it mean to you personally that God loves you so much that He sent Jesus to rescue you? Journal your response to God's goodness.

God rescued us from dead-end alleys and dark dungeons.
He's set us up in the kingdom of the Son He loves so much,
the Son who got us out of the pit we were in,
got rid of the sins we were doomed to keep repeating.

COLOSSIANS 1:13-14 THE MESSAGE

Forgiveness is a day-by-day, sometimes a moment-by-moment, process with God.

SUSAN GOSS

Faith, Love, and Forgiveness

Hearing that Jesus had silenced the Sadducees, the Pharisees got together.
One of them, an expert in the law, tested Him with this question:
"Teacher, which is the greatest commandment in the Law?" Jesus replied:
"'Love the Lord your God with all your heart and with all your soul
and with all your mind.' This is the first and greatest commandment.
And the second is like it: 'Love your neighbor as yourself.'"

MATTHEW 22:34–39 NIV

What a beautiful gift to have God's will for our lives boiled down to these two invitations: to love God first and then love our neighbors as ourselves.

What does it look like to love God with all our heart, soul, and mind? In part, it looks like faith. It takes faith to trust that God will do what He says He will do. Faith enables us to believe that God will help us forgive someone who has wronged us. Faith empowers us to release control to God and trust Him with the outcome.

We also fulfill these two greatest commandments by remembering that we love because God first loved us! (I John 4:19). And what is God's love like? His love is unconditional, steady, steadfast, and permanent. God's love never fails because God never fails and God *is* Love. In I Corinthians 13 we are told three things last forever: faith, hope, and love, but the greatest . . . is love!

We cannot fully receive God's love nor love others without forgiveness. Forgiveness allows the heart to feel free once again and brings healing to the soul. Forgiveness brings inner joy and peace where unforgiveness harbored bitterness, anger, and pain. Forgiving yourself or another is a faith journey we go through with a loving God holding our hand every step of the way.

Faith, love, and forgiveness are foundational in loving God supremely with all our heart, soul, and mind, which in turn strengthens us to love our neighbor. Being in relationship with others means we inevitably find ourselves in situations that require forgiveness—sometimes for the other person, sometimes for ourselves. When we recognize the incredible gift of God's forgiveness in our lives, we can live from a posture of grace.

There is a scene in the Bible that paints a vivid picture of the power of faith, love, and forgiveness. The story is about Jesus walking up to a woman who is drawing water out of a well at a most inconspicuous time of day, hoping to not be seen by anyone. Jesus, a Jew, is sitting at the well and kindly asks the Samaritan woman for a drink. At that time, this would have been culturally unacceptable on many levels. Jesus not only lovingly spoke with the Samaritan woman but also began telling her of things only she could have known about her current situation and her struggling past. Jesus offered unconditional love and forgiveness, and the woman had the faith to receive it. Instantly, a feeling of relief, acceptance, and joy drove the Samaritan woman to leave her jar of water and run back to town to tell others about everything that had happened to her. Because of her faith and because Jesus met her exactly where she was, loving her unconditionally and offering a forgiveness that brought freedom where shame had lived for so long, her powerful testimony brought many others to the same saving faith in Jesus.

We can entrust our entire lives to God!

Prompt to Ponder:

How did Jesus provide the Samaritan woman with all she would ever need? (Read John 4:7–30 for the full story.) How does this question apply to you?

And God will generously provide all you need.
Then you will always have everything you need
and plenty left over to share with others.

II Corinthians 9:8 nlt

Prompt to Ponder:

List the many ways that you overtly and covertly love God daily with your whole heart.

_____

_____

_____

_____

_____

_____

_____

_____

_____

_____

_____

_____

_____

_____

_____

_____

_____

_____

_____

_____

_____

_____

_____

_____

_____

_____

*"There is no greater love than to
lay down one's life for one's friends."*

JOHN 15:13 NLT

Prompt to Ponder:

How do you think the Samaritan woman felt after Jesus accepted her just as she was, forgave her sins, loved her unconditionally, and spoke truth over her that forever changed her life? What part of her story is your story too?

And may you have the power to understand,
as all God's people should, how wide,
how long, how high, and how deep His love is.

Prompt to Ponder:

How have you seen love cover offenses in your own life, either for an offense you committed or for an offense that someone committed against you?

_____

_____

_____

_____

_____

_____

_____

_____

_____

_____

_____

_____

_____

_____

_____

_____

_____

_____

_____

_____

_____

_____

_____

_____

_____

Hatred stirs up strife,
but love covers all offenses.

PROVERBS 10:12 NASB

Prompt to Ponder:

Is forgiveness something you do well? Or is it an area of struggle? Explain.

_____

_____

_____

_____

_____

_____

_____

_____

_____

_____

_____

_____

_____

_____

_____

_____

_____

_____

_____

_____

_____

_____

_____

_____

Don't retaliate with insults when people insult you.
Instead, pay them back with a blessing.
This is what God has called you to do,
and He will grant you His blessing.

I PETER 3:9 NLT

Prompt to Ponder:

How have you seen God's forgiveness work in your own life? How does this cause you to respond?

_____

_____

_____

_____

_____

_____

_____

_____

_____

_____

_____

_____

_____

_____

_____

_____

_____

_____

_____

_____

_____

_____

_____

_____

_____

Who is a God like you, who pardons sin and forgives
the transgression of the remnant of His inheritance?
You do not stay angry forever but delight to show mercy.
You will again have compassion on us; you will tread our sins
underfoot and hurl all our iniquities into the depths of the sea.

MICAH 7:18–19 NIV

Prompt to Ponder:

Knowing that everyone is our neighbor, journal your thoughts today about what it means to "love your neighbor as yourself." How can you do that well, as unto the Lord?

Let us hold tightly without wavering to the hope we affirm,
for God can be trusted to keep His promise.
Let us think of ways to motivate one another
to acts of love and good works.

HEBREWS 10:23–24 NLT

So we keep on praying for you,

asking our God to enable you to live

a life worthy of His call. May He give

you the power to accomplish all the good

things your faith prompts you to do.

Then the name of our Lord Jesus will be

honored because of the way you live,

and you will be honored along with Him.

This is all made possible because

of the grace of our God and Lord,

Jesus Christ.

II THESSALONIANS 1:11–12 NLT

The Comfort Promises by DaySpring™

No matter what you are facing today, you can rest in knowing the Creator of the universe loves you. He loves you deeply and perfectly with absolutely no conditions. And He's made hundreds of promises to you!

Below you'll find the 100 most referenced, quoted, and memorized Bible promises. At DaySpring, we call these The Comfort Promises™—the verses we turn to again and again for encouragement, joy, and strength.

For your convenience, we've provided a quick reference guide—a unique tool that makes it easy for you to find just the right comfort promises for your immediate need.

When you are AFRAID . . .

- He will not allow your foot to slip; He who keeps you will not slumber. PSALM 121:3 NASB

- Do not fear; I will help you. ISAIAH 41:13 NIV

- Draw near to God, and He will draw near to you. JAMES 4:8 CSB

When you are ANXIOUS . . .

- If you follow Me, you won't have to walk in darkness, because you will have the light that leads to life. JOHN 8:12 NLT

- Don't fret or worry. Instead of worrying, pray. PHILIPPIANS 4:6 THE MESSAGE

- He never changes or casts a shifting shadow. JAMES 1:17 NLT

When you need ASSURANCE . . .

- He is the faithful God, keeping His covenant of love to a thousand generations. DEUTERONOMY 7:9 NIV

- You're blessed when you're at the end of your rope. With less of you there is more of God. MATTHEW 5:3 THE MESSAGE

- He chose us...that we would be holy and blameless before Him. EPHESIANS 1:4 NAASB

- You are saved by grace through faith... it is God's gift. EPHESIANS 2:8 CSB

- He cares about you. I PETER 5:7 NLT

- His divine power has given us everything required for life. II PETER 1:3 CSB

When you need COMFORT . . .

- The LORD is near the brokenhearted; He saves those crushed in spirit. PSALM 34:18 CSB

- Take delight in the LORD, and He will give you your heart's desires. PSALM 37:4 CSB

- My faithful love for you will remain. My covenant of blessing will never be broken. ISAIAH 54:10 NLT

- I have it all planned out—plans to take care of you, not abandon you, plans to give you the future you hope for. JEREMIAH 29:11 THE MESSAGE

- He will rejoice over you with gladness...He will delight in you with singing. ZEPHANIAH 3:17 CSB

- Blessed are those who mourn, for they shall be comforted. MATTHEW 5:4 ESV

- He comforts us in all our troubles so that we can comfort others. II CORINTHIANS 1:4 NLT

- God has chosen you and made you His holy people. He loves you. COLOSSIANS 3:12 ICB

When you need COURAGE...

- But You, Lord, are a shield around me, my glory, and the One who lifts up my head. PSALM 3:3 CSB

- I can do all things through Christ because He gives me strength. PHILIPPIANS 4:13 ICB

- He hears their cry for help and saves them. PSALM 145:19 CSB

- I will strengthen you, I will help you, I will uphold you with my righteous right hand. ISAIAH 41:10 ESV

- This is what the Lord says, he who made the earth, the Lord who formed it and established it—the Lord is His name: "Call to Me and I will answer you and tell you great and unsearchable things you do not know." JEREMIAH 33:2–3 NIV

- The Lord is good to those who wait for Him, to the person who seeks Him. LAMENTATIONS 3:25 NASB

- I will send you the Helper from the Father. He is the Spirit of truth who comes from the Father. JOHN 15:26 ICB

- He hears us. I JOHN 5:14 NASB

When you need HOPE...

- The Lord will fight for you, while you keep silent. EXODUS 14:14 NASB

- Be strong; don't give up, for your work has a reward. II CHRONICLES 15:7 CSB

- The Lord grants favor and honor; He does not withhold the good from those who live with integrity. PSALM 84:11 CSB

- He has planted eternity in the human heart. ECCLESIASTES 3:11 NLT

- His mercies never end. They are new every morning. LAMENTATIONS 3:22–23 CSB

- I am the living bread.... Whoever eats this bread will live forever. JOHN 6:51 NIV

- Anyone who believes in Me will live, even after dying. JOHN 11:25 NLT

- We have this hope as an anchor for the soul, firm and secure. HEBREWS 6:19 NIV

When you need JOY...

- Do not grieve, for the joy of the Lord is your strength. NEHEMIAH 8:10 NIV

- You will fill me with joy in Your presence. PSALM 16:11 NIV

- You turned my lament into dancing. PSALM 30:11 CSB

- Give, and it will be given to you. LUKE 6:38 NIV

When you are LONELY...

- He will be with you; He will not leave you or abandon you. DEUTERONOMY 31:8 CSB

- The Lord your God is with you wherever you go. JOSHUA 1:9 CSB

- He Himself has said, "I will never leave you or abandon you." HEBREWS 13:5 CSB

When you are feeling OVERWHELMED...

- For nothing will be impossible with God. LUKE 1:37 ESV

- The God of all grace...will himself restore, confirm, strengthen, and establish you. I PETER 5:10 ESV

When you need PEACE...

- The Lord gives His people strength; the Lord blesses His people with peace. PSALM 29:11 CSB

- Peace I leave with you. My peace I give to you. JOHN 14:27 CSB

- God's peace will keep your hearts and minds in Christ Jesus. PHILIPPIANS 4:7 ICB

When you need PROTECTION...

- You are a hiding place for me; you preserve me from trouble. PSALM 32:7 ESV

- You protect people as a bird protects her young under her wings. PSALM 36:7 ICB

- God has not given us a spirit of fear, but one of power, love, and sound judgment. II TIMOTHY 1:7 CSB

- Humble yourselves before the Lord, and He will lift you up. JAMES 4:10 NIV

When you need ENCOURAGEMENT...

- His faithful love endures forever. PSALM 100:5 CSB

- I will be your God throughout your lifetime—until your hair is white with age. ISAIAH 46:4 NLT

- I will give you a new heart and put a new spirit within you. EZEKIEL 36:26 CSB

- For I am convinced that neither death nor life, neither angels nor demons, neither the present nor the future, nor any powers, neither height nor depth, nor anything else in all creation, will be able to separate us from the love of God that is in Christ Jesus our Lord. ROMANS 8:38-39 NIV

- He will not let you be tempted beyond your ability. I CORINTHIANS 10:13 ESV

- He has created us anew in Christ Jesus, so we can do the good things He planned for us. EPHESIANS 2:10 NLT

When you need FORGIVENESS...

- I will forgive their sin and will heal their land. II CHRONICLES 7:14 NIV

- Though your sins are scarlet, they will be as white as snow. ISAIAH 1:18 CSB

- By giving Himself completely at the Cross, actually dying for you, Christ brought you over to God's side and put your lives together, whole and holy in His presence. COLOSSIANS 1:22 THE MESSAGE

- He...will forgive us our sins and purify us. I JOHN 1:9 NIV

- God, who...will bring you with great joy into His glorious presence without a single fault. JUDE 1:24 NLT

When you need GUIDANCE...

- He will make your paths straight. PROVERBS 3:6 CSB

- The LORD will continually guide you. ISAIAH 58:11 NASB

- When the Spirit of truth comes, He will guide you into all truth. JOHN 16:13 NLT

When you need HEALING...

- He heals the brokenhearted and binds up their wounds. PSALM 147:3 ESV

- By His wounds we are healed. ISAIAH 53:5 NIV

- I will give you back your health and heal your wounds. JEREMIAH 30:17 NLT

When you need HELP...

- I will send you rain in its season, and the ground will yield its crops and the trees their fruit. LEVITICUS 26:4 NIV

- Day after day He bears our burdens. PSALM 68:19 CSB

- He will give His angels orders...to protect you in all your ways. PSALM 91:11 CSB

- The LORD will guard your going out and your coming in from this time forth and forever. PSALM 121:8 NASB

- He is a shield to those who take refuge in Him. PROVERBS 30:5 CSB

- A stronghold for the poor...a refuge from storms and a shade from heat. ISAIAH 25:4 CSB

- No weapon turned against you will succeed. ISAIAH 54:17 NLT

- He will strengthen you and protect you. II THESSALONIANS 3:3 NIV

When you need REST and RENEWAL...

- The LORD is my shepherd, I lack nothing. He makes me lie down in green pastures, He leads me beside quiet waters. PSALM 23:1-2 NIV

- He renews my life; He leads me along the right paths for His name's sake. PSALM 23:3 CSB

- He satisfies you with good things; your youth is renewed like the eagle. PSALM 103:5 CSB

- Those who wait for the LORD will gain new strength; they will mount up with wings like eagles, they will run and not get tired, they will walk and not become weary. ISAIAH 40:31 NASB

- Come to me, all who labor and are heavy laden, and I will give you rest. MATTHEW 11:28 ESV

- The Son of Man came to find and restore the lost. LUKE 19:10 THE MESSAGE

- Jesus answered, "Everyone who drinks this water will be thirsty again, but whoever drinks the water I give them will never thirst. Indeed, the water I give them will become in them a spring of water welling up to eternal life." JOHN 4:13-14 NIV

- Our inner person is being renewed day by day. II CORINTHIANS 4:16 CSB

- If anyone is in Christ, he is a new creation. II CORINTHIANS 5:17 CSB

When you need STRENGTH...

- He gives power to the weak and strength to the powerless. ISAIAH 40:29 NLT

- The Spirit helps us in our weakness. ROMANS 8:26 ESV

- He will keep you strong to the end so that you will be free from all blame on the day when our Lord Jesus Christ returns. I CORINTHIANS 1:8 NLT

When you are SUFFERING...

- He will sustain you; He will never allow the righteous to be shaken. PSALM 55:22 NASB

- As a father has compassion on his children, so the LORD has compassion on those who fear Him; for He knows how we are formed, He remembers that we are dust. PSALM 103:13-14 NIV

- I will be with you.... When you walk through the fire, you will not be scorched. ISAIAH 43:2 CSB

- I will be your God throughout your lifetime—until your hair is white with age. ISAIAH 46:4 NLT

- The LORD is good, a stronghold in the day of trouble. NAHUM 1:7 ESV

- Remain in Me, and I will remain in you. JOHN 15:4 NLT

When you need WISDOM...

- Continue to ask, and God will give to you. Continue to search, and you will find. Continue to knock, and the door will open for you. MATTHEW 7:7 ICB

- It is because of Him that you are in Christ Jesus, who has become for us wisdom from God—that is, our righteousness, holiness and redemption. I CORINTHIANS 1:30 NIV

- Now if any of you lacks wisdom, he should ask God...and it will be given to him. JAMES 1:5 CSB

When you are WORRIED...

- Your Father knows the things you need before you ask Him. MATTHEW 6:8 ICB

- God will meet all your needs. PHILIPPIANS 4:19 NIV

Faith Love Forgiveness: Devotional Journal
© 2024 Susan Goss. All rights reserved.
First Edition, June 2024

Published by:

21154 Highway 16 East
Siloam Springs, AR 72761
dayspring.com

All rights reserved. The *Faith Love Forgiveness: Devotional Journal* are under copyright protection.
No part of this journal may be used or reproduced in any manner whatsoever without written permission
except in the case of brief quotations embodied in critical articles and reviews.

Scripture quotations marked NASB1995 are taken from the NEW AMERICAN STANDARD BIBLE ®,
© Copyright 1960, 1962, 1963, 1968, 1971, 1972, 1973, 1975, 1977, 1995 by the Lockman Foundation.
Used by permission. (www.lockman.org)

Scripture quotations marked NASB are taken from the (NASB®) New American Standard Bible®,
Copyright © 1960, 1971, 1977, 1995, 2020 by The Lockman Foundation. Used by permission.
All rights reserved. www.lockman.org

Scripture quotations marked NIV are taken from THE HOLY BIBLE, NEW INTERNATIONAL VERSION®,
NIV® Copyright © 1973, 1978, 1984, 2011 by Biblica, Inc.® Used by permission.
All rights reserved worldwide.

Scripture quotations marked NLT are taken from the Holy Bible, New Living Translation, copyright ©
1996, 2004, 2015 by Tyndale House Foundation. Used by permission of Tyndale House Publishers, Inc.,
Carol Stream, Illinois 60188. All rights reserved.

Scripture quotations marked ESV are taken from the ESV Bible® (The Holy Bible, English Standard
Version®) copyright ©2001 by Crossway Bibles, a publishing ministry of Good News Publishers.
Used by permission. All rights reserved.

Scripture quotations marked CSB are taken from the Christian Standard Bible®, Copyright © 2017 by
Holman Bible Publishers. Used by permission. Christian Standard Bible® and CSB® are federally registered
trademarks of Holman Bible Publishers.

Scripture quotations marked THE MESSAGE are taken from THE MESSAGE, copyright © 1993, 1994, 1995,
1996, 2000, 2001, 2002 by Eugene H. Peterson. Used by permission of NavPress.
All rights reserved. Represented by Tyndale House Publishers, Inc.

Scripture quotations marked TPT are from The Passion Translation®. Copyright © 2017, 2018 by Passion &
Fire Ministries, Inc. Used by permission. All rights reserved. ThePassionTranslation.com.

Scripture quotations marked TLB are taken from The Living Bible copyright © 1971. Used by permission
of Tyndale House Publishers, Inc., Carol Stream, Illinois 60188. All rights reserved.

Scripture quotations marked The Voice are taken from The Voice™.
Copyright © 2012 by Ecclesia Bible Society. All rights reserved.

Written by: Susan Goss
Cover Design: Becca Barnett

Printed in China
Prime: U2769
ISBN: 979-8-88602-872-0